Make Time 4 Love

21-Day Devotional for Couples

Dawn2Dawn Publishing

8810C Jamacha Blvd #136

Spring Valley, CA 91977

ISBN: 978-0-9914000-1-0 (sc)

ISBN: 978-0-9914000-0-3 (e)

The views expressed in this work are solely those of the author and do not necessarily reflect the views of the publisher, and the publisher hereby disclaims any responsibility for them.

Published by Dawn2Dawn Publishing 2017

FOREWORD

In today's society, marriages face several obstacles that cause couples to look for ways to stay inspired and in-love. This 21-Day Love Devotional will prompt you to become the spouse that God requires. Its instructional approach to daily living will bring discipline and maturity to your marriage.

As our spiritual children in the Gospel, we are excited to see how Earnest and Fidelia Dawn have penetrated the heart of a healthy relationship through this 21-Day Love Devotional. Being an experienced minister has afforded Earnest Dawn with an aptitude for getting in touch with God to garner an extensive understanding of the scriptures. As a seasoned author, Fidelia Dawn's eloquent writing style allows the reader to capture inspiration through imagery and dialogue.

This combination of gifts has brought about topics that will inspire and motivate couples into establishing time, respect, value, and consideration for each other. The benefits of this 21-Day Love Devotional are extraordinary.

Suffragan Bishop, Dr. William A. Benson
First Lady, Dr. Rachelle Y. Benson

Day 1: Partners in Battle

Deuteronomy 32:30
How should one chase a thousand, and two put ten thousand to flight, except their Rock had sold them, and the LORD had shut them up?

Ephesians 6:12
For we wrestle not against flesh and blood, but against principalities, against powers, against the rulers of the darkness of this world, against spiritual wickedness in high [places].

As individuals, we are up against the rulers of darkness of this world. These forces want to kill, steal, and destroy us, as well as everything we hold dear. Together, a husband and wife are the strongest and most effective. The enemy knows that when couples join forces, get on one accord, and battle together, his agenda doesn't stand a chance. His first step in destroying the Church is to destroy the family unit. He does that by cultivating discord within the marriage. He takes the battle, which should be outwardly directed at him, and inverts it. Disagreements and personality differences become the ammunition for war, and before long, a marriage turns into a casualty beyond repair. So, link up with your spouse and battle as allies, not enemies. Together, we overcome more, achieve more, and conquer more.

Notes

_____

_____

_____

_____

_____

_____

_____

_____

_____

_____

_____

_____

_____

_____

Notes

_____

_____

_____

_____

_____

_____

_____

_____

_____

_____

_____

_____

_____

_____

_____

_____

_____

Day 2: Don't Hold Back

I Corinthians 7:2-5
2 Nevertheless, [to avoid] fornication, let every man have his own wife, and let every woman have her own husband. 3 Let the husband render unto the wife due benevolence: and likewise also the wife unto the husband. 4 The wife hath not power of her own body, but the husband: and likewise also the husband hath not power of his own body, but the wife. 5 Defraud ye not one the other, except [it be] with consent for a time, that ye may give yourselves to fasting and prayer; and come together again, that Satan tempt you not for your incontinency.

There are times when being together intimately is not feasible, but what about the other times?

Honoring this scripture can be difficult, especially when interactions with your spouse have been less than ideal. The reality of every marriage is that there will be trying times, but working on continuously nurturing an atmosphere of wooing your spouse makes submitting to their physical needs a pleasure, not a hardship.

Wooing entails more than being wined and dined extravagantly. It is being a partner, going the extra mile to ease each other's burden. It is being a comforter and friend, a source of positivity amongst the negativity in each other's lives. In doing this, climbing into bed together isn't overshadowed by the man who forgot your birthday or the woman who hung up on you when you needed to talk. You'll see the love of your life—the one who bought you flowers or cooked your favorite meal when you were having a rough day. Submitting to their physical needs is a breeze when you don't have days' worth of discontentment to forge through.

Withholding intimate contact puts a divide in the union, leaving space for the enemy to set up camp. In that space, the enemy will plant temptation, feelings of inadequacy, resentment, unfulfilled urges, a wandering mind, and so much more. All of these agents can destroy a marriage.

Notes

_____

_____

_____

_____

_____

_____

_____

_____

_____

_____

_____

_____

_____

_____

_____

Notes

_____

_____

_____

_____

_____

_____

_____

_____

_____

_____

_____

_____

_____

_____

Day 3: Get Home Right First

Matthew 5:23-24

23 Therefore if thou bring thy gift to the altar, and there rememberest that thy brother hath ought against thee; 24 Leave there thy gift before the altar, and go thy way; first be reconciled to thy brother, and then come and offer thy gift.

Pause. Whatever work you are doing for the Kingdom—whether you're singing, preaching, teaching, or ushering—it can *all* wait. How can you minister or work in the Kingdom while simultaneously giving your spouse the silent treatment? Ignoring issues and allowing them to fester while going on like nothing's happened is just like leaving food rotting in the refrigerator. At first, the food looks all right; you can still eat it if you want. Before long, it starts to stink. You open the refrigerator and the odor fills the house. The stench gets worse, and before long, nothing can be done and you have to throw out the entire dish. Unresolved issues may seem minor, but they can erode a marriage until it's irreparable.

On the other hand, you don't want lingering issues to hinder the move of God. When you get up to minister or offer your gift, let there be nothing hindering you or threatening to destroy your effectiveness.

Notes

Notes

Day 4: Motivate Each Other

Hebrew 10:24-25

24 And let us consider one another to provoke unto love and to good works: 25 Not forsaking the assembling of ourselves together, as the manner of some [is]; but exhorting [one another]: and so much the more, as ye see the day approaching.

If we don't know how to do anything else, we know how to push our spouse's buttons. Why not use that power for good? If we learn what upsets them, we can figure out how to encourage them. We pray and seek the Lord for a word to uplift our brothers and sisters in Christ, but why not our spouse? A positive word from the one you love can last a lifetime.

In these end times, we are facing a world full of hardened hearts and stony faces shooting daggers with their tongues. A smiling face from our mate can erase all opposition. Make time to encourage, motivate, uplift, and speak to their heart.

We should know their calling and their gifts. Let that be the point where you provoke them to achieve their goals. Push them out of their comfort zone(s)! What greater feeling than to see your spouse's accomplishments and know you were a part of them.

Notes

_____

_____

_____

_____

_____

_____

_____

_____

_____

_____

_____

_____

_____

_____

Notes

Day 5: Submit to Your Husband

Colossians 3:18
Wives, submit yourselves unto your own husbands, as it is fit in the Lord.
Ephesian 5:2
And walk in love, as Christ also hath loved us, and hath given himself for us an offering and a sacrifice to God for a sweet-smelling savour.
I Peter 3:1
Likewise, ye wives, [be] in subjection to your own husbands; that, if any obey not the word, they also may without the word be won by the conversation of the wives;

Submission and subjection—in the world of today's modern woman—holds such a negative connotation. Women have fought for equality, and the thought of surrendering what generations have strived for can seem to knock the women's rights movement back a few decades. But, looking more deeply at what those words mean brings about a better understanding of the scripture.

Submit: to accept or yield to a superior force; or, to present to a person for consideration

Subjection: being under one's power and authority

These words are not used to diminish who a woman is or hinder her accomplishments, but they are to establish biblical order within a marriage. I Peter 3:7 refers to the wife as the *weaker vessel*.

Vessel: object used as a container

Women try to contain it all: the weight of the family, finances, children, and even their extended families. They've got it all under control and try to bear it alone, but if a woman yields to the superior force, which is her husband, she won't have to contain so much. The overwhelmed, frazzled, overworked woman will cease to exist. Being the weaker vessel or submitting to your husband does not mean you're weak, needy, or dependent. It means you weren't built to withstand it all alone and you acknowledge that you don't have to.

A wife surrendering to her husband's authority reveals that she trusts him. It shows she believes in him and has faith that he has everything under control. This knowledge can propel a man forward, change the way he sees himself, and bring about an even closer relationship with the Lord. He will not take advantage of her trust, but will value it.

Notes

Notes

Day 6: Love as Christ Loves the Church

Ephesians 5:25
Husbands, love your wives, even as Christ also loved the
church, and gave himself for it.

Colossians 3:19
Husbands, love [your] wives, and be not bitter against
them.

When you consider how Christ loves the Church, the call to be a husband can be an intimidating responsibility. Christ's love toward the Church is longsuffering; it endures all, never fails, is all-consuming, and is unconditional. The Church, as well as your wife, can be a bit temperamental, but the love of Christ and her husband surpasses her emotional, moody, volatile persona. It is the love of Christ that draws, embraces, and comforts. Husbands, be that type of love for your wife. When you lose sight of the extraordinary way the Lord loves you, it is easy to become bitter about your spouse. That is where the enemy would have you stay. Just remember, she is the gift God has given you and she deserves the same love Christ has shown to you.

In addition, wives, Christ loves the Church. Never take that love for granted and expect it to always be there when you are not appreciating it. There is a point where even God takes His love away.

Notes

_____

_____

_____

_____

_____

_____

_____

_____

_____

_____

_____

_____

_____

Notes

Day 7: Self-Control

I Thessalonians 4:4
That every one of you should know how to possess his vessel in sanctification and honour;

Titus 2:5-8
5 [To be] discreet, chaste, keepers at home, good, obedient to their own husbands, that the word of God be not blasphemed. 6 Young men likewise exhort to be sober minded. 7 In all things shewing thyself a pattern of good works: in doctrine [shewing] uncorruptness, gravity, sincerity, 8 Sound speech, that cannot be condemned; that he that is of the contrary part may be ashamed, having no evil thing to say of you.

As a Christian and as a spouse, self-control is important. Once you say "I do," your life is no longer just about you. Your actions and the words that come out of your mouth indirectly affect your spouse. You can no longer be a loose cannon or engage in some of the activities you enjoyed while single. Self-control and maintaining sound Christian character is not taking away your identity or trying to change you into something you are not. It is merely you governing yourself, being discreet, and remaining sober-minded. There are things which are expedient for the single Christian that a married individual should abstain from. Always put the shoe on the other foot. How would you feel if your spouse did or said what you are getting ready to?

Notes

_____

_____

_____

_____

_____

_____

_____

_____

_____

_____

_____

_____

_____

_____

Note

_____

_____

_____

_____

_____

_____

_____

_____

_____

_____

_____

_____

_____

_____

Day 8: Become One

Mark 10:8-9
And they twain shall be one flesh: so then they are no more twain, but one flesh. 9 What therefore God hath joined together, let not man put asunder.

Genesis 2:24
Therefore shall a man leave his father and his mother, and shall cleave unto his wife: and they shall be one flesh.

Oftentimes the word 'one' is centered on living space, finances, and activities. It is thrown into arguments and used as ammunition to get a spouse to become more considerate. Some even dread the word *one* in relation to marriage. It is seen as diminishing a person's individuality.

Let's look a little deeper at *one*. Before marriage, you were—one single, solitary digit—one mind, personality, passion, goal, dream, and calling. You were all that by yourself, and marriage shouldn't diminish that. What it does is enhance all that you are. Two minds conjoin to focus on life. Two personalities team up to make life interesting. Two passions merge into a blazing inferno that's impossible to extinguish. Two sets of goals and dreams combine to push each other and make success all the more possible. Two callings unite to form an unstoppable force in the Kingdom. When two blend into one, they do not lose themselves in the process. They become bigger, better, and stronger.

Notes

_____

_____

_____

_____

_____

_____

_____

_____

_____

_____

_____

_____

_____

_____

_____

Notes

Day 9: Respect Your Man

Esther 1:20
And when the king's decree which he shall make shall be published throughout all his empire, (for it is great,) all the wives shall give to their husbands honour, both to great and small.

Ephesians 5:33
Nevertheless let every one of you in particular so love his wife even as himself; and the wife [see] that she reverence [her] husband.

Respect: esteem for or a sense of the worth or excellence of a person; favor or partiality

Whether a man is a millionaire or a stay-at-home dad, he is worthy. Whether a minister or lay member, he is worthy. Respect is not tied up in financial contributions, college degrees, or job titles. Respect and honor him simply because he is YOUR husband. What if he chose not to love you because you didn't work, couldn't cook, or couldn't have children? He'd be called all kinds of names, and your friends and family would tell you to leave him. But, a man is expected to just sit and take disrespect? Just as a woman needs love, a man needs respect. Respect from his wife when the world is beating him down can be the driving force that keeps him pressing forward. Respect is not bowing down, taking abuse, and turning a blind eye to infidelity. It is simply saying, "You, my husband, are the head of this house. I honor your opinion, trust you to make decisions for us, and will walk by your side while we follow Christ." Have esteem for his worth and the excellence that's in him.

Notes

Notes

Day 10: When the Storm is Raging

Proverbs 31:10-12

Who can find a virtuous woman? for her price [is] far above rubies. 11 The heart of her husband doth safely trust in her, so that he shall have no need of spoil. 12 She will do him good and not evil all the days of her life.

A woman is a powerful force. She can destroy a man or build him up with merely the words that come out of her mouth. If she seeks to harm her husband, she will be successful. She'll blow through his mind, self-esteem, and his heart like a hurricane, leaving only destruction in her wake. She can utterly destroy him, but when she flows in her gift, striving to put her power to good work, she will be like the eye of a storm. The world can be raging all around, his life spiraling like a tornado, but with and through her, he can find peace. Don't jump into the storm and be a part of his stress; be his center.

Notes

Notes

Day 11: Love Abounds

I Thessalonians 3:12-13
And the Lord make you to increase and abound in love one toward another, and toward all [men], even as we [do] toward you: 13 To the end he may stablish your hearts unblameable in holiness before God, even our Father, at the coming of our Lord Jesus Christ with all his saints.

Philippians 1:9-11
And this I pray, that your love may abound yet more and more in knowledge and [in] all judgment; 10 That ye may approve things that are excellent; that ye may be sincere and without offence till the day of Christ; 11 Being filled with the fruits of righteousness, which are by Jesus Christ, unto the glory and praise of God.

There are many things in life toward which we have affinity. We have a natural, almost innate gravitation toward things we love. Some love their jobs, and in essence, become workaholics. Some love their children and dote on them until they're spoiled rotten. Others love their things: houses, cars, electronics, and many other material possessions. Of all the things we love, our love for one

41

another should abound. Your love should overflow and grow, not diminish. Falling out of love takes a conscious effort of neglecting what's important. Learn how you need to be loved and how your spouse needs to be loved. There shouldn't be any guessing; speak and listen. Hear your spouse's needs, speak your own, and then make it your mission to give and be open to receive.

Notes

_____

_____

_____

_____

_____

_____

_____

_____

_____

_____

_____

_____

_____

_____

_____

Notes

Day 12: No Looking Back

Philippians 3:13-14

Brethren, I count not myself to have apprehended: but [this] one thing [I do], forgetting those things which are behind, and reaching forth unto those things which are before, 14 I press toward the mark for the prize of the high calling of God in Christ Jesus.

When two imperfect people come together with different thoughts, desires, ideals, and morals and conjoin their lives, there are bound to be mistakes made. Feelings will get hurt. There will be disappointments and disagreements. Living in anger, holding grudges, and sleeping on the couch isn't a solution. It's a conduit to heartache. It's not God's will for you to live in misery.

No one has arrived at perfection, so show some grace and mercy to your spouse. At some point, you have to let it go and let it stay gone. Once you move past a rough patch, let it stay in the past and keep moving forward. Looking back or bringing up situations that have already been resolved takes you back into that moment of heartache. If you're not careful, you'll find yourself cycling through the same problems over and again.

46

Notes

_____

_____

_____

_____

_____

_____

_____

_____

_____

_____

_____

_____

_____

Notes

Day 13: Love and Respect

Ephesians 5:28, 33
28 So ought men to love their wives as their own bodies. He that loveth his wife loveth himself. ... 33 Nevertheless let every one of you in particular so love his wife even as himself; and the wife [see] that she reverence [her] husband.

With the same thoughtfulness and thoroughness you care for your own body, you should consider your wife. You make sure you have what you need, even splurge on a few luxuries. You're well fed. You drink water, exercise, get haircuts, bathe, and dress yourself up. Making sure your wife is taken care of and feels loved is like taking care of yourself. Some might say, "You're spoiling her; you're the man," or "She needs to tend to me," but she needs that affection to feel appreciated. When a wife receives such selflessness, she will reciprocate and give her man the love and respect he needs. You, as the man and head of the house, making an effort to love that which the Lord has entrusted to you will set up you and your household to be blessed.

Notes

_____

_____

_____

_____

_____

_____

_____

_____

_____

_____

_____

_____

_____

_____

_____

Notes

Day 14: Prayer and Supplication

Ephesians 6:18
Praying always with all prayer and supplication in the Spirit, and watching thereunto with all perseverance and supplication for all saints;

Philippians 4:6
Be careful for nothing; but in everything by prayer and supplication with thanksgiving let your requests be made known unto God.

Prayer is the key to the presence of God. It gets His attention and shows signs of faith. By seeking to pray, you inadvertently acknowledge God as the Supreme Being and the solution to your life. Healing, guidance, deliverance, restoration, peace, and everything you need in life becomes attainable through prayer. What's so common is, people will pray for the sun and the moon before they'll pray for their marriage. When things get tough, marriage is thrown out like yesterday's garbage. *I don't have time for his shenanigans. I love her, but I have to be me. I can do bad all by myself. What's the point in being married if he/she is not going to help me?*

We've just grown apart. A relationship with the Father will bring any wall or mountain down. It will cause the raging seas to cease and be still upon speaking and declaring in the Name of Jesus! Why not direct all that power toward our marriages? Prayer changes things and can change what's wrong in a marriage if we diligently seek the Lord. Go in with a humble heart and willingness to change. Don't give up! Fight through prayer!

Notes

Notes

Day 15: He Will Rebuke the Devourer

Malachi 3:10-11

10 Bring ye all the tithes into the storehouse, that there may be meat in mine house, and prove me now herewith, saith the LORD of hosts, if I will not open you the windows of heaven, and pour you out a blessing, that [there shall] not [be room] enough [to receive it]. 11 And I will rebuke the devourer for your sakes, and he shall not destroy the fruits of your ground; neither shall your vine cast her fruit before the time in the field, saith the LORD of hosts.

Money issues can destroy a marriage. The stress and struggle of juggling the bills around your paydays and falling short each month can take its toll. That's when the finger pointing and accusing your mate of being the source of the problem usually begins. The problem is greater than them. Your finances are being devoured. Being faithful in your giving will motivate God to rebuke mindsets and actions that are devouring your finances. Take God at His word, give, and it shall be given back. Not only can faithful giving increase your income, but it will also change your mind set about money and spending habits, and before long, things will line up. Finances won't be depleted by the end of the month.

Giving is a faith walk. It takes faith to take money from an already insufficient budget and give it away. You could probably come up with ten other, seemingly more beneficial, uses for the money, but TRY HIM. Little becomes much when you place it in His hands.

Notes

Notes

Day 16: The Little Foxes

Song of Solomon 2:15
Take us the foxes, the little foxes, that spoil the vines: for our vines [have] tender grapes.

Your lives are filled with busy schedules. You work, you go to church, you minister, you go to school, and you have kids. Through all of that, sometimes you get tired. You let things slip through the cracks. You don't pray. You take a few Sundays off from church. You let little white lies slip. Before long, you've slipped into your old habits. Just as little things can hinder your spiritual walk, the little neglected things in a marriage can have big consequences. You fall short on tasks and lie to cover it up. You forget a birthday, put off date night, or don't take time to show appreciation. You forget about loving your spouse the way you should. You don't give them the things they need: affection, support, respect, companionship, and compliments. The lack of these—what some may see as minor things—will work like little foxes and destroy what has been built. One little thing can fester into years of discontentment. You have to watch out for those little foxes. Don't let them steal or destroy your love, joy, peace, happiness, and ultimately, your marriage.

Notes

Notes

Day 17: Something New

I Corinthians 5:6-7

6 Your glorying [is] not good. Know ye not that a little leaven leaveneth the whole lump? 7 Purge out therefore the old leaven, that ye may be a new lump, as ye are unleavened. For even Christ our passover is sacrificed for us:

Isaiah 43:18-19

18 Remember ye not the former things, neither consider the things of old. 19 Behold, I will do a new thing; now it shall spring forth; shall ye not know it? I will even make a way in the wilderness, [and] rivers in the desert.

Purge the old to make room for the new. No one is perfect, and some have made damaging mistakes. You or your spouse may have lied, been neglectful, and maybe even cheated. A marriage can survive all of that and then some, but you have to purge the pain. These negative things happen in marriages, and you try to move forward; however, when there's a disagreement or another issue, it's brought up again. It's because someone is still holding on to the pain of past mistakes. They're afraid to let the pain go, because they're afraid of being vulnerable. It's a defense mechanism used to block the blow of future indiscretions.

God can do a new thing, so push forward from the past. The former things are done and gone, so invest your time, energy, and efforts into the future. You have to purge that pain to make room for the renewed love, commitment, and joy that's trying to get in. It takes work, prayer, fasting, and willingness from both parties, but you must also keep looking unto Jesus, the author and finisher of your faith.

Notes

Notes

Day 18: Turn the Other Cheek

Matthew 5:38-39

38 Ye have heard that it hath been said, An eye for an eye, and a tooth for a tooth: 39 But I say unto you, That ye resist not evil: but whosoever shall smite thee on thy right cheek, turn to him the other also.

How many times have you done something without thinking of the consequences? Transgression is like a slap in the face to God, and His mercy is Him turning the other cheek. He spares us from the slap back we deserve. God's had so much patience with all of us. As we indulged in the sin, He could've said, "Time's up," and issued judgment. He didn't give the immediate reprimand we deserved—the immediate reprimand we so frequently give to our spouse. "I am done with you" or "I can't do this anymore" is not the solution to every argument. You are going to have bad days. Instead of being confrontational and escalating the situation, turn the other cheek and address the situation while everyone is level-headed.

Notes

Notes

Day 19: Say What You Mean

Matthew 5:37

But let your communication be, Yea, yea; Nay, nay: for whatsoever is more than these cometh of evil.

A baby comes into this world with the sounds of crying, grunts, and laughter. No one understands what they are trying to communicate. Parents have to guess what their babies want. As they get older, they develop language and perfect how to express their needs, fears, and desires. Adults regress. In spite of the years they've spent developing and perfecting dialogue, they refuse to use it. Communication is an enormous obstacle in marriages. The silent treatment, assuming they already know, speaking in codes, and dropping hints only accentuates conflict. Use your words! Tell your spouse how you really feel. How will they know something they are doing is upsetting you if you don't tell them? They are not mind readers. Also, open your ears to listen. Communication is sending and receiving messages. Your reception has to be just as good as your sending.

Notes

Notes

Day 20: Do Unto Others...

Matthew 7:12
Therefore all things whatsoever ye would that men should do to you, do ye even so to them: for this is the law and the prophets.

It's simple: if your spouse treated you the way you treat them, would you be happy?

It is important to evaluate your relationship and give what you expect to receive. Any marriage rooted in the 'eye for an eye' principle is doomed to fail. Someone has to rise up and stop the tit for tat, 'you got me, so I'm going to get you back' mentality. Try seeking to please and see how rewarding it feels when that smile spreads across our spouse's face.

Don't expect more than you are willing to give. In the event it seems as though you're giving more than you get or you're treating them the way you want to be treated and it's one sided, it is not going unnoticed by the other party. Remember, prayer changes things.

Notes

Notes

Day 21: You Shall Reap

Galatians 6:9
And let us not be weary in well doing: for in due season we shall reap, if we faint not.

Trust and believe that applying all these principles will positively affect your marriage. Change is hard, especially when you're fighting against forces that so desperately want you to fail. But, greater is He that is within you. You are more than a conqueror. God is on your side. A fulfilling marriage is His will. So, don't get weary! Keep fasting, praying, fighting, pressing, and persevering. YOU SHALL REAP IF YOU FAINT NOT!!!

Notes

Notes

_____

_____

_____

_____

_____

_____

_____

_____

_____

_____

_____

_____

_____

_____

_____

www.ingramcontent.com/pod-product-compliance
Lightning Source LLC
Chambersburg PA
CBHW050549280326
41933CB00011B/1775